QUIT PULLING MY LEG!
A Story of Davy Crockett

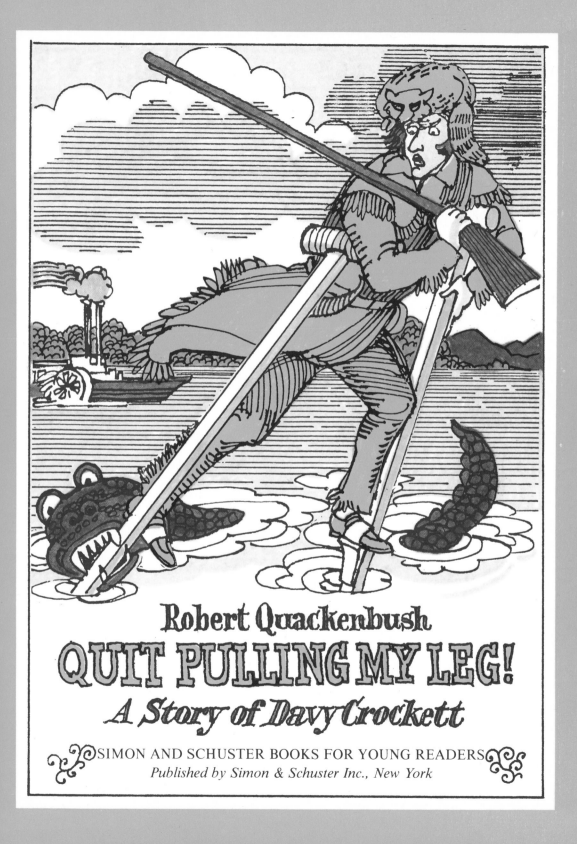

Robert Quackenbush

QUIT PULLING MY LEG!
A Story of Davy Crockett

SIMON AND SCHUSTER BOOKS FOR YOUNG READERS
Published by Simon & Schuster Inc., New York

SIMON AND SCHUSTER
BOOKS FOR YOUNG READERS
Simon & Schuster Building
Rockefeller Center
1230 Avenue of the Americas
New York, New York 10020
Copyright © 1987 by Robert Quackenbush
All rights reserved
including the right of reproduction
in whole or in part in any form. ˙
SIMON AND SCHUSTER BOOKS FOR YOUNG READERS
is a trademark of Simon & Schuster Inc.
Printed in Spain by Novograph, S.A., Madrid.

10 9 8 7 6 5 4 3 2
10 9 8 7 6 5 4 3 2 1 (Pbk)

Library of Congress Cataloging-in-Publication Data
Quackenbush, Robert M.
    Quit pulling my leg! A Story of Davy Crockett
    Summary: A brief illustrated biography of the renowned
American frontiersman.
    1. Crockett, Davy, 1786-1836—Juvenile literature.
2. Pioneers—Tennessee—Biography—Juvenile literature.
3. Tennessee—Biography—Juvenile literature.   4. Legis-
lators—United States—Biography—Juvenile literature.
5. United States. Congress. House—Biography—
Juvenile literature.   [1. Crockett, Davy, 1786-1836.
2. Pioneers.   3. Frontier and pioneer life]   I. Title.
F436.C95Q33   1987   976.8′04′0924   [B]   86-21795
ISBN 0-671-66516-2   ISBN 0-671-69441-3 (Pbk)

There was once a boy named David Crockett. He was born August 17, 1786 in a log cabin in the wild frontier country of Tennessee. Davy—as he was to be called, though he never called himself by that name—had five brothers and three sisters. The family was very poor and everyone had to pitch in and do a share of the farm work and hunting in order to survive. At the age of three, Davy learned to use a bow and arrow. He dreamed of being a great hunter. One day he went into the woods full of daring. He shot an arrow at a small bear. The arrow merely poked the animal but it made him very angry. Davy had to run for his life.

LOOK! I FOUND THIS OLD ALMANAC. IT TELLS ALL ABOUT DAVY CROCKETT. WHEN HE WAS A BABY, HE SLEPT IN A 12-FOOT-LONG CRADLE MADE FROM THE 600-POUND SHELL OF A SNAPPING TURTLE.

YOU'VE GOT TO BE KIDDING!

From that day Davy realized that in order to be a good hunter, he must know the ways of the wild frontier. Every day he went deep into the woods. He learned to imitate the calls of birds and the sounds of animals. He learned to track game as silently as an Indian. Soon he was bringing home wild game and fish for the dinner table. But food was not all that the family lacked. They needed new clothes for one thing, and decent tools for another. At last, when Davy was seven, his father gave up the struggle to provide for his large family by hunting and farming. He opened a small inn on the Wilderness Trail that ran from Virginia to Eastern Tennessee. Traders and hunters came to the inn. After meals the men would tell fantastic tall tales—or "leg pullers," as they called them —about their adventures. Davy listened and then made up tall tales about his own adventures. "Let me tell you how I tamed a passel of wild snakes, panthers and tigers till they were all licking my hands," he would begin. As he told his tale, his listeners howled with laughter.

10

Davy's knowledge of the wilderness and his ability to tell tall tales were tested to the fullest when he was twelve. A cattle-driver named Mr. Siler paid Davy's family in advance to have Davy help him drive a herd of cattle to northeast Virginia—400 miles away. It took them five months to get there. When the cattle were sold, Siler forced Davy to stay and keep working for him. Afraid of Siler's anger, Davy pretended he was willing to stay. He entertained Siler with his tall tales. All the while he kept looking and waiting for a chance to escape. Then one night, during a snowstorm, Davy managed to get away by climbing out a window while Siler slept. He trudged seven miles through knee-deep snow for hours until he came to a camp. There he met a man with a wagon who knew his father and happened to be going to Tennessee. He took Davy safely home.

The following fall, Davy was sent to school for the first time. He wanted no part of it. He could not see what it had to do with hunting and fishing. So after only four days in school, Davy was ready to leave home again. He heard about a neighbor who was also driving a herd of cattle to Virginia and was looking for someone to help on the journey. Davy ran away to join him. When they reached Virginia and the cattle were sold, Davy decided to stay and see the country. He drove a plow, harvested crops, and even worked as a hatmaker. Two years later he headed back home. No one in the family recognized the young man of fifteen who came strolling into the inn. He had changed greatly from the boy who had left so long ago. It was only when everyone sat down to dinner that his older sister looked at Davy and exclaimed, "Here is my long lost brother!"

15

Davy was very glad to be home. For a while he hired himself out to neighbors to pay the debts his father owed them. Then he decided to go back to school. He found farm work that would allow him to attend school four days a week. By the time he was seventeen, he had learned to read, write, and spell. He had also saved enough from his wages to buy his first rifle, which he named "Old Betsey." Davy would not part with his rifle for anything in the world. He spent all his spare time in the woods, practicing with Old Betsey. When he was ready, he entered shooting matches—a popular sport on the frontier. He won all of them. People traveled for miles to see Davy Crockett shoot the wick of a lighted candle at 300 yards. Stories about his feats spread far and wide. They grew into tall tales that were told about him around campfires across the land.

17

After the shooting matches, play-parties were often held. These were dances where couples swung each other arm-in-arm while a fiddler played tunes like "Skip-to-my-Lou." In 1805, when he was nineteen, Davy met Polly Finley at a play-party. She was the daughter of a new settler from North Carolina. Davy began to court Polly and two months later she agreed to marry him. They began housekeeping in a deserted cabin with $15.00 worth of groceries and supplies given to them by a storekeeper. When three months had passed, Davy convinced Polly that they should move farther west where the land was good and the hunting was even better. So they moved on to Southern Tennessee. Davy cleared a patch of ground and raised corn, potatoes, beans, and other vege-tables. Old Betsey provided plenty of wild meat for their meals. It was a good life, and within a few years, two sons were born to the Crocketts.

18

Then, in 1813, when Davy was twenty-seven, a neighbor brought news: Creek Indians had massacred some white settlers at Fort Mims in Alabama. General Andrew Jackson, who commanded the militia in Tennessee, called for volunteers to fight the Creeks. Davy filled his saddlebags with food, strapped Old Betsey across his back, mounted his horse, and rode off to enlist. He fought the Creeks on horseback along with 1300 other frontiersmen. Davy distinguished himself by his bravery under fire. He rejected an offer to become a commissioned officer, saying, "A title don't mean nothin'." General Jackson said, "Davy Crockett provided a bountiful supply of meat for my forces. He was the merriest of merry; keeping the camp alive with his wit and marvelous narratives." Just as he had since he was a little boy, Davy continued even in time of war to provide meat for the table and to bring cheer with his tall tales.

20

About six weeks after a peace treaty with the Creeks was signed on August 10, 1814, some of the Creeks fled to Pensacola, Florida. They did not want to submit to the terms proposed in the treaty. But the War of 1812 was still going on. The Spanish, who then ruled Florida, allowed British soldiers stationed there to train the Creeks for an invasion of New Orleans. Once again, General Jackson called for volunteers, this time to fight the British in Florida, and Davy reenlisted. But after the capture of Pensacola, Davy received word that his wife was seriously ill. He returned home at once, but a month later Polly died, leaving him with two sons and a baby daughter. Then Davy roamed Tennessee for months, seeking a new place to live. When he finally settled, he met a young widow, Elizabeth Patton, whose husband had been killed in the Creek War. She had a son and daughter. Soon Elizabeth and Davy were married and the children of both parents were united under one roof.

Davy's new life included a new home for his family in West Tennessee that was seven miles from his nearest neighbor. It was in the heart of bear country! One day he arrived at a trading post with 105 bear skins. People were amazed. "I ain't feared of nothin' that breathes," said Davy. Then he told some tall tales about how he had tracked the bears, and how he had made a pet of a bear he named "Death Hug." Everyone loved Davy's yarns. They also liked his generous nature, for he was always ready to turn over his best catch of the day to someone who needed it more than he did. People believed that he was a spokesman for the common man. They began talking about sending him to Congress to represent West Tennessee.

At first Davy laughed at the notion of being a Congressman. Then when he thought about it some more, he came to the decision that it was his duty to go to Washington and represent his people. He began to campaign for votes. He made people laugh with his backwoods stories and they called him "Colonel" Crockett. He would climb on a stump and say, "I am like a fellow I heard of not long ago. He was beating on the head of an empty barrel near the roadside, when a traveler who was passing along asked him what he was doing. The fellow replied that there was cider in that barrel a few days ago, and he was trying to see if there was any left, but if there was he couldn't get at it. There was a little bit of a speech in me a while ago, but I don't believe I can get it out." The people gathered around would roar with laughter, and then Davy would go on to tell them what he could do for them in Washington. His campaign was successful and he was elected to Congress from West Tennessee in 1827.

In Washington, people laughed at his backwoods manners. Some called him "the gentleman from cane," making fun of his home in one of Tennessee's then-poor rural backwaters where sugar cane grew. Davy turned the insult into a compliment. He deliberately cultivated the image of an uneducated but honest backwoodsman who possessed common sense, as most of the people he represented believed themselves to be uneducated but honest. However, he did not wear the clothes of a backwoodsman in Washington. Dressed in a formal suit, he stood before Congress and said, "I say, Mr. Speaker: I can outspeak any man on this floor and give him two hours start. I can outlook a panther, outstare a flash o' lightnin', tote a steamboat on my back, and play at rough and tumble with a lion. I can walk like an ox, run like a fox, spout like a volcano, and swallow a man whole if you butter his head and pin his ears back." Davy was letting them know that he was a man of action and that he would not sit back and be an observer during his term of office.

29

When Andrew Jackson was inaugurated President, in 1829, Davy Crockett supported him at first. That was because Davy had served under him during the Creek War and also because they were both from Tennessee and both represented the common man. But soon Davy disagreed with Jackson over two pieces of legislation that Davy bitterly opposed. One was a Public Lands Bill which would prevent poor people from homesteading—or working on the land without paying for it—in certain parts of Tennessee. The other bill would let the government take back land it had given to Indian tribes and move the tribes to new areas. Davy believed the bill would violate a treaty the government had made with the Indians. By the early 1830's Davy had joined the Whig party which opposed Jackson. However, the people in Tennessee were all for the President. Davy was warned that if he didn't support Jackson, he might not get re-elected. Davy's always rosy cheeks glowed even brighter. "Who cares?" he said. "Then I'll go home and hunt bear."

ANDREW JACKSON

By this time the adventures of Davy Crockett were known across the land. He had more followers than you could imagine. He was elected for Congress three times (in 1827, 1829, and 1833) and defeated only once (in 1831). He held the office a total of six years. Wherever he traveled, he was welcomed as a national hero. In New York, he was presented with the latest model rifle with engraved silver mountings; in Boston, factory girls threw him kisses; in Baltimore, he was wined and dined by important people; in Philadelphia, he was invited to speak at fancy banquets. Then in 1835, Davy entered the race for Congress for the fifth time. The Jackson supporters made extra efforts to defeat Davy. Their candidate won after a bitter campaign. "Politics can go to blazes," said Davy afterwards, "I'm going to Texas."

32

True to his word, Davy did go to Texas which was then part of Mexico. While he was looking for land where he could settle, he became involved in the Texas struggle for independence. He enrolled as a volunteer soldier to fight the Mexican army. In February, 1836, at the age of forty-nine, he joined the small band of brave men who fought to save the Alamo, a fortress at San Antonio. The defenders were defeated by Mexican soldiers who outnumbered them by more than thirty to one. Davy Crockett was one of the few survivors taken prisoner, and he was put to a torturous death by sword. The news of his heroism moved the nation deeply. His widow was given 1500 acres of Texas land. Davy himself left behind two possessions for his heirs. One was a gold watch. The other was a copy of Ben Franklin's *Autobiography*. In the front of the book, Davy had written:

> *I'll leave this truth for others when I am dead.*
> *Just be sure you are right and then go ahead.*

Epilogue

The same year Davy Crockett fell at the Alamo, he became a legendary folk hero. This happened when an enterprising Nashville publisher printed the first issue of "Davy Crockett's Almanack." Along with the usual almanac information about weather and crops, it contained illustrated stories that expanded wildly on his exciting exploits. There were wonderfully impossible accounts of Davy scrapping with panthers and bears, sinking pirate ships, and outwitting everyone from Indians to redcoats. As a result of these almanacs, which were sold all over the world, David Crockett the man became Davy Crockett the myth. It may even be that he never wore a coonskin cap! The legend of Davy Crockett has been portrayed for over a century in books, in plays, and on our television and movie screens. It appears that, like all myths that tell us about an era or a culture, the Legend of Davy Crockett will live forever.

36